COPY 65

745.54   JOHNSON, Lillian (Bass)
PAPIER-MÂCHÉ.   New York, McKay, 1958.

Related⎤
Books in ⎟   88p.   illus.   3.95
Catalog ⎬   1. PAPIER MACHÉ
Under ⎦

'68

N 62

Papier-Mâché

Papier-Mâché

by LILLIAN JOHNSON

DAVID McKAY COMPANY, INC.

New York

Library of Congress Catalog Card Number 58-9802

Manufactured in the United States of America

Van Rees Press • New York

To My Husband, LEO JOHNSON

CONTENTS

Papier-Mâché

The unlimited possibilities of papier-mâché remain very much a mystery in the craft field, in spite of its simple method and inexpensive and easily available supply of materials. In its simplest form it can be used by young children to make masks, puppets, and other craft projects. By perfecting techniques, it can be used as a creative means of expression; another form of sculpture. It is a quick technique, requiring simple materials, and it needs very little work space.

In the many years of working with papier-mâché I have discovered many variations of techniques and means of achieving textural effects. Many of these methods are secrets closely guarded by papier-mâché artists in the professional display field. I do not propose to divulge all these variations, but will present the most basic methods of construction with a few variations. Once you have mastered these, it is up to you to put your ingenuity to work to create interesting ideas and novel and individual effects.

3

MASKS

There are two basic methods of mask making. Anyone attempting to work as a papier-mâché artist should first learn to make a mask. That way you learn:

1. What paper can do.

   Always remember that YOU are the master and paper must do your bidding. Properly handled, paper is a willing slave.

2. How to mix paste and make paper sticky enough to behave.

3. How to interlock paper strips for strength, and proper coverage for enough body.

4. To understand the shrinkage possibilities.

5. To experiment with finishing techniques.

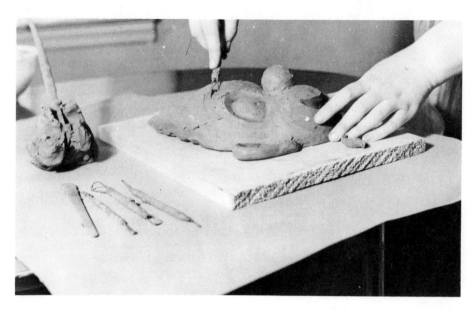

THE POSITIVE METHOD

Begin by building a clay mask like the paper one you want to make.

Plasteline is recommended for this, for it is a waxlike clay that never hardens, and may be used and reused for years. If this is not available, ordinary wet clay will do. Plasteline or wet clay can be bought at any art or hobby supply store.

Prepare a bowl of paste. A good paste can be made with wheat paste (wallpaper paste) that can be purchased in any hardware or paint store. Follow the directions on the package. To be most effective, the paste should be about the consistency of thick pea soup. Library paste thinned with water can also be used.

8

Prepare the paper by tearing it into strips about one inch to an inch and a half wide. Paper must always be torn, not cut. The ragged torn edges help to bind the strips to each other more smoothly. Many kinds of paper can be used. Newspaper works very well, with the advantage of being always available. It lacks only weight. Paper bags or paper toweling can also be used. An excellent all-around paper that serves well for papier-mâché is bogus paper, a soft absorbent paper often used for packing dishes and glassware. This paper usually has to be bought from wholesale paper distributors who do not wish to sell small quantities, so it is a good idea to try to collect it from packings when only small quantities are needed. Another good

source of paper is wallpaper. Leftover wallpaper rolls are found in many cellars, and wallpaper sample books may often be procured from your local paint and wallpaper dealer, who discards them after each season.

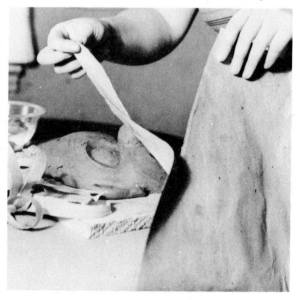

Papier-Mâché

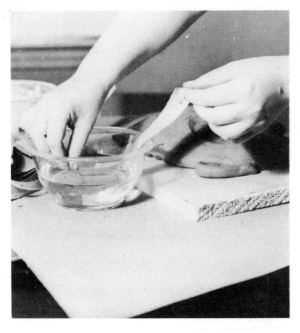

Now the ground-work is laid and you are ready to make a mask. The first layer of paper strips is wet but not pasted, so that the paper will not stick to the clay. The wet strips are laid on the clay and gently molded over the forms.

As much as possible, have strips interlock so that each strip crosses over another one at some point. This is important to give the mask strength without too much weight.

10

When the mask is entirely covered with the first layer of wet strips, continue the same process with three or more layers with pasted strips. It is wise, whenever possible, to use different  colors on alternate layers to be sure that the coverage is even and that no spot remains neglected. When using newspaper, for example, every other layer can be made from the colored comic section. When using wallpaper, put one layer color side up, and the next one color side down.

 Be sure to keep molding the paper over the forms of the mask as you go along layer after layer, so that none of the forms are obscured by the paper. Three layers of paper were used on this mask. In this case bogus paper was used. With lightweight paper such as newspaper six or more layers may be needed.

11

Papier-Mâché

After the final layer has been completed, let the paper set. It should be dry or almost dry before it is lifted off the clay model. If it is taken off too wet, it might distort or shrink during the drying process. This is particularly true if drying is forced. Whenever possible, allow the paper mask to dry naturally.

After the mask is dry, trim the edges with scissors or a sharp craft knife.

The mask is now ready to be painted.

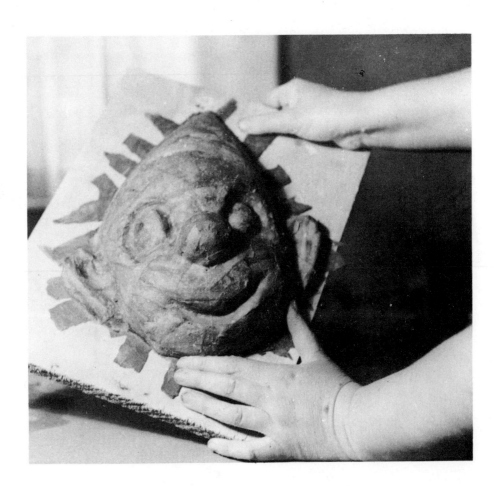

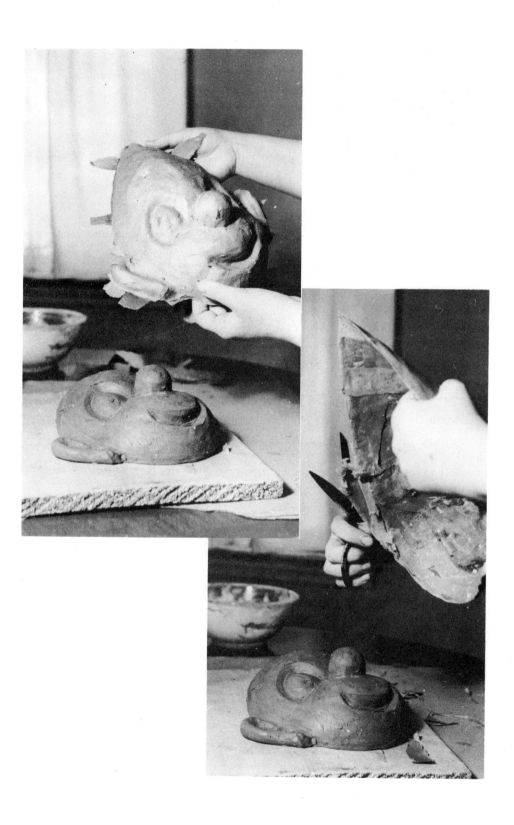

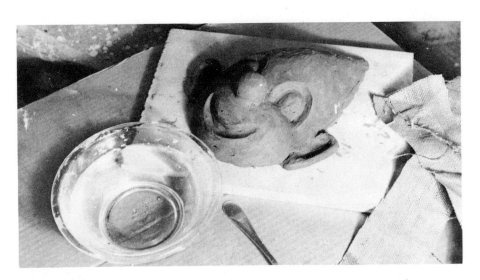

THE NEGATIVE METHOD

This method is the reverse of the positive method. Instead of building the papier-mâché over the clay model, a plaster cast is made of the clay, and then any number of papier-mâché copies can be made by pressing the paper into the plaster cast.

If the model is made from plasteline, no separator is necessary.

If it is made from any other material, it is necessary to use a separator to keep the plaster from sticking to the model. This may be done by any one of the following methods:

An application of liquid soap with a soft brush.

An application of oil or vaseline, or a similar substance. If the model is porous, give it a coat of shellac first, then oil.

An application of sodium silicate (known as water glass).

14

Mix a bowl of plaster. Use casting plaster, or plaster of Paris, which can be bought in small quantities at an art and handicraft store, or in larger amounts at a hardware store or lumber yard. Fill the bowl half full of water. Into this sift the plaster by handfuls until small islands of plaster no longer sink into the water. Stir gently to break up any lumps. Then, working quickly, apply the plaster by spoonfuls to the model. Be sure to get plaster in all the details. Gently tap the table or board

under the model to help the plaster flow into all the forms and to bring any air bubbles to the surface. Continue adding plaster for strength. The plaster should be between one inch to one inch and a half thick.

15

Papier-Mâché

The thickness of the plaster mold can be cut down if strips of burlap are dipped into the plaster and laid across the first layer of plaster after all the details are well covered and the plaster has begun to hold its shape. Cover the burlap strips with a thin layer of plaster. This makes a clean, strong mold.

Let the plaster set thoroughly before attempting to separate it from the clay. Plaster has a chemical action which cannot be hurried.

The plaster will become quite warm and then cool off. Do not disturb it until it has cooled. To be on the safe side, allow more than an hour before separating the plaster from the clay.

Carefully remove the clay.

We now have a negative, or a reverse of the model. Clean out the plaster mold and smooth out any unnecessary roughness with a knife.

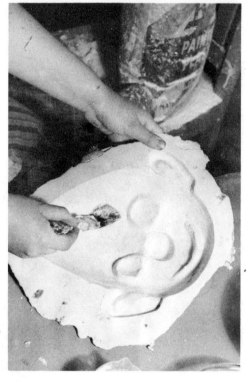

Paint the inside of the mold with liquid soap until it is thoroughly saturated. This gives the mold a slippery surface which helps prevent the paper from sticking to the plaster.

17

Papier-Mâché

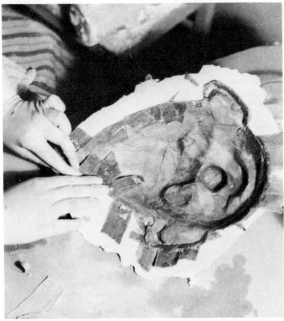

Proceed with the same steps as in the positive method, only in reverse. Instead of putting paper strips on a model, the paper strips are molded into the negative forms of the mold. It is a good idea to have the strips extend about an inch beyond the mold. The first layer is not pasted on the side that touches the mold.

In this case three layers of paper are used. The ends are then folded back to make a clean and strong edge. Or the rough edge may be left to be trimmed later with scissors or a sharp knife.

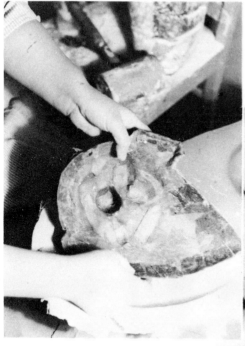

The paper should be set, although it need not be dry, before it is lifted from the mold.

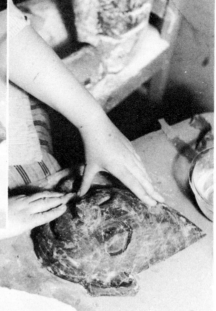

If the paper strips have been well interlocked the mask will lift out easily.

Handle it gently. If it is too wet the paper will pull out of shape. Rub or brush paste on the mask to secure any loose strips. The mask is now ready to dry.

There are several advantages to the negative method:

1. The duplication of forms is more exact.

2. The mold may be used innumerable times, making it possible to produce quantities of the same mask.

3. It can be stored away for any length of time and is always ready to use.

COLOR
TEXTURE
AND TRIM

Whether you have used the positive or the negative method, you now have a basic mask. Now is the time really to put your imagination to work.

The number of variations in color alone is countless.

There are several possible ways to paint papier-mâché. Tempera paints, poster colors, or casein paints are most often used. These paints are water soluble, and good for mixing any colors and shades you might desire. Casein paints have the advantage of being more permanent than the other two types of paint, and the colors will not bleed through. (Bleeding refers to the color of an undercoat showing through or coloring any coat of paint that is put over it.) It is also possible to paint a light color over a dark color with casein, something that is difficult to do with poster paint. Casein and poster paint mix well together, so a quantity of white casein and a collection of small jars of poster paint will go a long way toward solving the color problems of papier-mâché.

Sometimes it is necessary to protect the finished paint on papier-mâché. This can be done by painting a coat of clear shellac over it, or if you wish to weatherproof it, use two or three thin coats of shellac. Be sure each coat is thoroughly dry before applying another. Clear varnish, laquer, or one of the commercial sprays can also be used.

Papier-Mâché

If an oil-paint finish is preferred, be sure to give the paper surface a coat of shellac before using the oil paint. Otherwise the paper will absorb the oil in the paint, and the resulting effect will be uneven and dull.

If a smooth surface is required, rub the paper gently with sandpaper before painting. Or paint it first with a thin solution of jointing cement and white casein. This will give the paper a good painting surface.

Before you consider your papier-mâché project ready for color, consider the possibilities. Suppose the mask is a clown as in the illustration. Has it character? Can you create more interest with texture? What trimmings will help convey his personality? Put your imagination to work. Make a collar and pompon of tissue paper, crepe paper, or even cloth net in gay colors. Make some of the colors theatrical by sprinkling sparkle (known also as glitter or diamond dust) or sequins over the paint while it is still wet. Or make a gay polka-dot bow tie and hat band to match. Ransack a button and ribbon drawer, or take the trim off some old hats. Hair textures can be created by using wool or cotton yarn which can be pasted into place in curls, braids, or general confusion. Or the hair can be made of papier-mâché, and for this tissue paper or crepe paper produces the best results.

Sparkle and sequins can be bought at most art and handicraft stores.

24

To illustrate some of the possible variations, I have taken a number of copies of the mask that has been made in the mold just described. By varying collars, ties, hats, and hair, each mask becomes an individual. In this case nothing but paper and paste are used. Tufts of hair are made with tissue paper made quite sticky with paste. Hat effects are achieved mostly by adding a brim. Here this is done with strips of bogus paper which are trimmed to shape. The collars are shaped and folded fairly dry, then secured with pasted strips to the back. Bow ties are made of folded strips of paper tied as regular bows. The feather is cut paper. A piece of wire holds it erect.

25

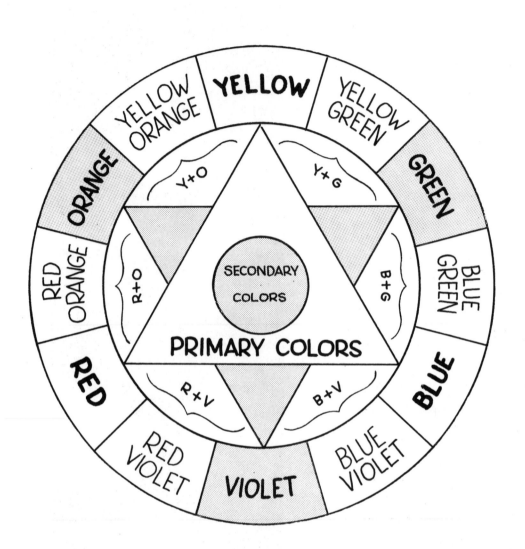

Color, Texture, and Trim

Some basic information about color mixing:

There are three **primary** colors: yellow, red, and blue.

A **primary** color is basic, and cannot be made by a mixture of any other colors.

Two **primary** colors mixed together will produce a **secondary** color. Hence yellow and blue make green; red and yellow make orange; and red and blue make violet.

The three **primary** colors, or the three **secondary** colors, mixed together, neutralize one another.

Colors directly opposite each other on the color wheel are called **complementary** colors, as red and green, orange and blue, yellow and violet.

Complementary colors mixed together make gray.

Warm colors are those containing yellows and reds.

Cool colors are the blues and greens.

Skin colors can be mixed by adding orange to white.

To mix a pale color, or a tint, always add the color slowly to white. Never add white to the color, or you may end up with ten times more paint than you need.

Papier-Mâché

Hue refers to the pure color.

Value refers to the shade of the color from light to dark. White or black added to the color changes the color value.

Chroma refers to the intensity of the color, from bright to neutral. The complement of a color added to it will reduce its intensity.

Colors often suggest meaning and emotion:
  Cool colors are quiet.
  Warm colors are gay.
  Red and green immediately suggest Christmas.
  Orange and black means Halloween.
  Pastel colors are associated with spring and Easter.
  And so on—.

Now armed with this basic information, three jars of primary colors, three jars of secondary colors, some black and white paint, and several assorted brushes, you are ready to tackle the color problems of any papier-mâché project.

Color, Texture, and Trim

Now you know how to make papier-mâché masks—but do not stop there. It is possible to make many objects for decorative or display purposes; all kinds of forms in the half round, human or animal, or purely imaginative. It can be used to make puppet heads or for making paper-craft projects for scouts or similar groups of children at recreation centers or camps.

There is another thing to know related to mask making before we go on to direct papier-mâché. That is how to put two pieces together to make a full round, such as a front and back of a head as in making a puppet.

If only one head is needed, the simplest method would be to make the clay head in the full round and work the paper strips all around it. Then, when the paper is thoroughly dry, cut away a section in the back, or slice it with a razor to divide the head in half, to remove the clay. The two pieces can easily be put together with pasted strips.

Papier-Mâché

If a quantity of full round heads is needed, it is best to make a front and back plaster mold. This is done by dividing the original clay model into two convenient sections and making a plaster mold of both the front and the back. Make the division by inserting thin pieces of metal, aluminum or brass, into the clay. Cover with plaster as described in the negative mask method (see page 14). Leave the top ends of the metal exposed. When the plaster is set, pull out the metal pieces with a plier. This will separate the mold into two pieces.

The paper is laid in both the front and back molds. Trim the edges carefully so the two pieces will fit together when dry. The edges will merge better if they are not entirely dry, so it is helpful to dampen them with some thin paste. Whenever possible, seal the seams with well-pasted strips from the inside. However, it is possible to paste the strips on the outside to merge the seam so that it can't even be found. When dry, sandpaper will complete the job.

This process will be more fully explained in the section about the full-round figure (see page 33).

This half-round figure was designed as an advertising symbol for a YWCA annual fund-raising project. Several plaster molds were made from the original clay model. The papier-mâché work was done by a group of volunteer women who had never done this kind of work before.

THE FULL
ROUND FIGURE

We come now to the more creative phase of papier-mâché—individual figures built around an armature. There is practically no limit to the possibilities in this field. You can work on any scale, from miniature to gigan-  tic; for fine details or large cartoon effects; for small decorative figures or weatherproof monuments. These figures are made in the full round so they may be seen complete from any direction.

For a small figure about twelve inches high, a simple wire armature is needed. The armature is equivalent to a skeleton, and similar to a stick figure.

Practice with pipe cleaners to learn proportions and to see how much action you can get. Try some of these; then vary the poses. Often the pipe-cleaner poses will suggest an interesting idea.

Papier-Mâché

The surest way of getting just what you want in the papier-mâché is to design your figure first on paper. Draw it actual size. The wire can then be measured and bent to the correct size and action right against the drawing.

36

The Full Round Figure

Buy galvanized wire at a hardware store. Judge the gauge (thickness) so that the wire is flexible enough to bend, but rigid when assembled. A wire cutter and a plier complete the necessary equipment.

There are no rules to cover armature making. Everyone will find his own pet method. However, a very simple way to start is to cut one long piece of wire which will, when bent in the center, make the head, body, and legs. Twist the bend to form a loop for the head. Then another long piece twisted under the head loop forms the arms. Animal armatures can be made with three pieces of wire: one to make front and back left legs; one for front and back right legs; and one long one with loop at the end to make the head, neck, back, and tail. After the wire is bent to the correct action, it can be nailed to a board to make it self-

standing. It may be nailed securely so that the board becomes a permanent base for the figure, or it may be tacked temporarily so that the board may be removed later.

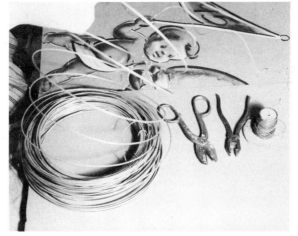

Papier-Mâché

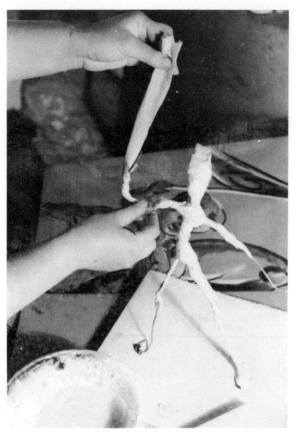

To begin the papier-mâché, assemble the paper and a bowl of paste. Since the paper is wrapped around and around the armature, it should be of the soft variety, such as newspaper, tissue paper, or paper toweling. The figure illustrated is made with tissue paper. The paper is made slightly sticky with paste and then wrapped around the wire. Do not make the paper too wet with paste or the figure will become sodden and difficult to handle. Also, the wetter the paper, the more it shrinks when drying.

Now that there is a wrapping of paper all around the armature, begin to add more paper for added bulk. Work toward the final shape of the figure.

It is a good plan to let it dry after several layers, for as it dries, it hardens. It will be easier to handle and form if the undercoats are dry. The finished forms will shape better with well-pasted strips.

38

Small wads of soft paper help to build out the forms such as the cheeks and tummy. Notice how the strips follow the direction of the form. Let the strips spiral and cross each other as much as possible.

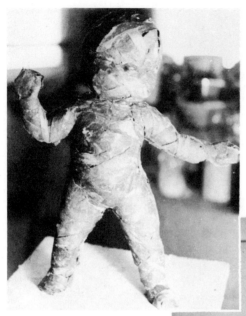

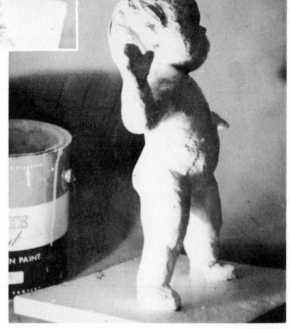

For most purposes the paper will dry smoothly enough, but if a smoother surface is required, paint the figure with a thin coat of spackle or jointing cement, which can be bought in small quantities at a paint or hardware store. When this is dry, the figure can be sanded. Now you are ready to paint.

40

The Full Round Figure

For costumed figures, it is possible to get big effects like a full gathered skirt by using larger pieces of paper, made slightly sticky with paste. Gather and drape it just as in dress-making. This technique is good for shapes like pants, sleeves, aprons, etc. Treat trimming such as ruffles and bows as though they were cloth. Wet it, shape it, then paste it on.

· There are a great many ways to get textural effects. Many of these will have to be invented as the need arises. But here are some suggestions:

1. An animal can be made to look furry by puckering the paper or pinching it while wet. For this, tissue paper is ex- cellent.

2. For long, shaggy-hair effects, shred the ends of the paper before pasting, leaving the shredded ends free.

3. Hair on small papier-mâché people can be made very styl- ish by shaping curls, braids, or any appropriate hair style with crepe paper or tissue paper and paste. Curl the paper around your finger or braid it just the way you would hair. Adjust the curls or braids with straight pins which will hold the paper hair in place until it is dry. Then the pins may be removed if they show.

4. Lacy edges may be added to dresses by using paper-lace doilies.

A group of dancing figures in costumes from many lands designed for a window display.

These figures, twelve inches high, are built around the simple wire armature just described.

Small animals are also made over a simple wire armature. The rough, uneven texture of tissue paper gives a furry look. The antlers of the deer are made of pipe cleaners, which are shaped, painted, and sparkled white.

43

These little angels were used in a series ot store windows to create a Yule spirit. The figures were made over the simple wire armature, but because there were about twenty of them, a mold was made for the face. This saved time, and made for more consistency. The hair was fashioned out of tissue paper. Ear muffs were crocheted angora. Wings were cut out of screening wire bent to shape, painted white, and sprinkled with white sparkle. A very soft angelic look was created by gently rubbing pastels (colored chalks) over the painted figures. This was done with the finger tips and blended with wads of cotton. The snow was salt.

Papier-Mâché

Now we are ready to work with the most flexible method of papier-mâché. The armature is made of chicken wire. This makes it possible to work on small round figures from about a foot in size up to gigantic figures of any size, providing they have wood or metal reinforcements inside.

The principle used is the same as in the wire-stick armature. The difference is that now we replace solid masses of paper by forming an approximate figure out of chicken wire around which the papier-mâché is shaped. This results in a very durable figure that is light at the same time. This has many advantages. For example, a papier-mâché prop in a theater can be made to look dense and heavy, but can be easily lifted and moved about for quick scene changes. A papier-mâché manikin is

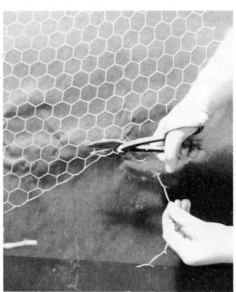

light and durable, yet even a six-foot figure could float gracefully in the air suspended by a few wires.

Again, begin with a full-size drawing. For the armature buy some one-inch mesh chicken wire and a wire cutter at the lumber yard or hardware store.

Clip off the hard end.

The Full Round Figure

Look at the drawing as parts made up of a series of cylinders of various dimensions to make arms, legs, body, etc. Now cut the chicken wire so that, when it is bent and the cut ends interlocked, it will form cylinders the right length and circumference to make these body parts.

Experiment with the wire until you discover its flexibility for shapes. Bend it. Stretch it. Squeeze it. When the arms bend at the elbow, and waists are pinched in, and legs bend at the knees, assemble the parts.

Papier-Mâché

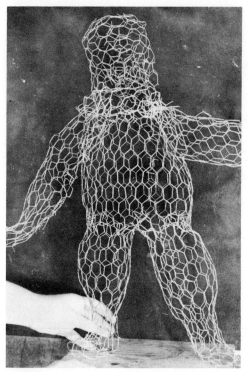

Interlock the cut ends to join two pieces. For a figure up to three feet no other support is necessary. When it is fully assembled and the action of the figure is right, it is usually helpful to nail the figure to a board to make it self-standing. The board may be removed when the figure is completed.

For figures over three feet high, an added support will be needed to keep the figure from sagging. This can be done with lengths of wood which are nailed to the base board and placed within the cylinders. Either nail or wire the chicken wire to the wooden support. Inexpensive lengths of lathe can be bought at a lumber yard to be used for the support. Be sure the wire armature has the right proportions, the proper action, and the approximate shape.

Get paper and paste ready.

The Full Round Figure

Depending, of course, upon the size of the figure you wish to construct, tear the paper into workable strips or squares. Some artists find it convenient to stack a quantity of sheets of paper each of which has been painted with paste (use a wallpaper brush). The paper is then torn off as it is needed. Although newspaper or craft paper are possible, it is more desirable to use a heavier bogus-type paper or wallpaper, particularly for working the basic shapes. A good heavy and pliable paper is building felt, which can be bought at a lumber yard or hard-

ware store by the roll. It will last for dozens of mâché figures and it is worth getting. The chicken-wire armature provides the basic strength of construction, so the paper is applied primarily for shape. There are no rules now for the number of layers to use. As the shapes and textures are determined, the construction takes care of itself.

Large bogus-paper strips make the basic shapes on this Santa Claus. The texture of the beard and mustache and the fur trim on the suit are added with tissue paper. The bottom flare of the coat and the belt are added last. Notice how simple the forms are kept. Paper lends itself to details, but too much of this will create only confusion.

Let the figure dry overnight before giving it the finishing touches. Natural drying is always best. However, in an emergency, drying can be forced by directing artificial heat evenly on the figure. An infrared lamp is particularly good for this purpose for it has a deep penetrating heat. If many layers of paper

50

were used and the figure is slow drying, poke a few holes in the figure to allow the moisture to escape from the inside.

Now consider the textural effects. Often a rough, casual effect is desirable. However, sometimes smoother surfaces are needed, as for faces. Again, as described for painting masks, paint the surface with a thin coat of jointing cement, or white casein paint, or a combination of both. When dry, go over the surface lightly with sandpaper. You are ready to paint.

Papier-mâché is hard on good brushes, so for most brush painting use the less expensive bristle brushes. Don't resort to the very cheap variety or you will leave a trail of brush hairs all over the painted surface. Reserve the finer brushes for the detail work. For this, use the round pointed camel-hair or sable brushes. Never let casein dry on the brush. Rinse it frequently in water.

Papier-mâché figures, like cartoons, can be painted with large areas of flat color, no shading, and very little detail. They can be painted casually for suggested effects.

Papier-Mâché

Or they can be painted quite realistically with careful attention to details. As in painting a picture, or creating a sculpture, the end result should be an effective individual expression.

Since papier-mâché figures are often used for display, for theatrical purposes, or for gay holidays, it is often necessary to glamorize them. Sparkle comes in many colors and adds a very theatrical quality. Sprinkle the sparkle lightly on the paint while it is still wet. White sparkle has a fairy-like quality. Colors may be dry brushed over one another to create depth, high lights, or just to give more life to the colors. A coat of varnish will make black boots look like patent leather. Faces come alive when a little rouge made with ground pastel colors is applied with soft wads of cotton. This process is also used to get muted tones in the folds of clothes. So you can see the possibilities are really unlimited, and it's very gratifying to see what you can produce.

O COME ALL YE FAITHFUL

This all-girl orchestra is made of papier-mâché figures about three feet high. The musical instruments are a combination of paper board and papier-mâché. They are surrounded by a light puff of cloud which is angel hair (spun glass).

Papier-Mâché

The diagrams show the armatures used for these angels. The gowns are tissue paper; the hair, crepe paper; the wings are screening cut and bent to shape, sprayed, and glittered white. The angels were painted white and, when thoroughly dry, delicately tinted with ground pastels rubbed on with soft cotton wads. The halos are wire with glitter.

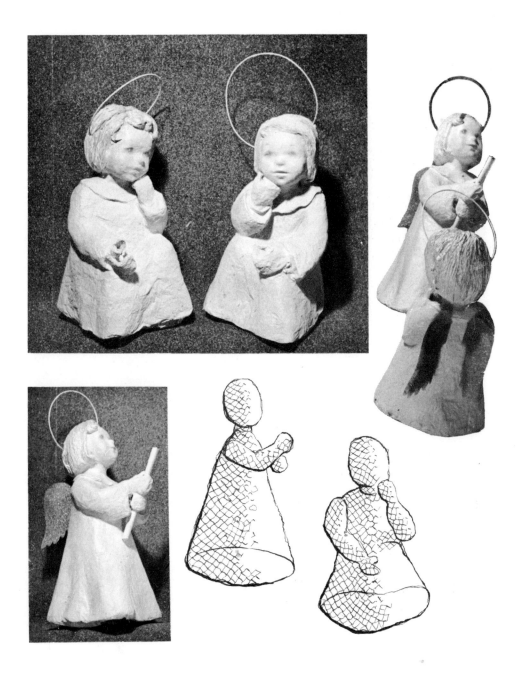

A gauzelike fabric is draped over the papier-mâché figures.

MERRY CHRISTMAS

The choir singer pictured above has hair made with strips of colored construction paper. A pencil or dull knife blade drawn the length of the strip of paper will make it curl.

Braided hair is made with crepe paper and paste.

The bell ringer is made with bogus paper over the simple tubular armature. The texture of the fur on the hat and coat is created by pinching and puckering tissue paper made sticky, but not soggy, with paste.

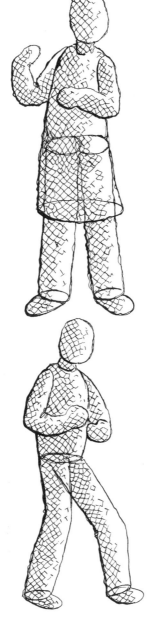

When doing a costumed figure, make an attempt to be accurate. Illustrated books on costuming through the years and in many countries are available in most public libraries. The public is quick to notice costume errors.

57

Costumes and customs of Mexico in this scene are fairly authentic. Notice the jug, also made of papier-mâché.

Papier-Mâché

This sketch of a snow man was submitted to a display director and approved. He wanted a number of them about two feet high in a variety of poses. In order to make this a full-round figure, a clay model was made first. The clay was divided into two sections by inserting pieces of aluminum in a crownlike fashion all around the side. The figure was then completely covered with plaster, leaving only the ends of the aluminum exposed. Burlap strips reinforced the plaster mold. When the mold was set, the aluminum strips were removed with a plier. The mold thus separated into two sections, a front and a back.

60

Now the process is exactly the same as in making a mask, only here two pieces were made, a front and a back. When the two pieces of papier-mâché dried, they were removed from the mold and put together. This was done by brushing the edges with paste and securing with strips of paper to conceal the division.

Using only one two-piece mold, more than a dozen different poses of the snow men were made. The variations were made after the snow men were put together and dry. By cutting the joint with a sharp craft knife, it is possible to tilt the head, raise an arm, change a position of the legs, etc. This change of pose is made permanent with more pasted strips. Hats were made directly on each man with paper cylinders, paper strips, etc.

Papier-Mâché

The snow men were painted with white casein and sprinkled liberally with white sparkle. The black coals for eyes, nose, mouth, and buttons were effectively created by sprinkling blue mica flakes over the wet black paint. Scarves were bits of flannel and felt. (They could also have been made of papier-mâché.) Other accessories came from the five-and-ten, toy bin, attic, Christmas boxes, etc.

These fat little fellows decorated the children's floor of a department store.

PUPPETS

Making puppets is great fun. Children at camps, in school, scouts, church schools, etc., love to create puppet plays. Here is a method so simple that any child eight years and up can create his own puppet.

There is, of course, the method described, which is to make the head first with clay. Cover the clay with paper strips (about five layers of newspaper). When dry, cut open, remove the clay, and paste together again with more strips.

Here is a method much quicker and easier.

But wait! Before you go any further, make sure you know what you will do. Will you make a comic head? A weird one? A clown? A devil? It would be a good idea to draw several pictures first. Experiment with character and expressions until you know just what you want.

Now you are ready to begin. The materials are simple. You need tissue paper, newspaper, paste, and poster paints. For the hollow neck, where the index finger holds the puppet head, use a paper roll like those found inside a roll of toilet tissue or paper toweling.

Over this roll, tissue paper is wrapped loosely and almost dry. Use just enough paste to hold it together. Build up the tissue paper until it is the general shape of the head. It is best to let this much dry. If you don't use too much paste, tissue paper will dry quickly.

Papier-Mâché

When the general shape has hardened enough to handle, the features can be put on. Again use tissue paper, only this time use small pieces and lots of paste. Add bits and pieces to build up a nose, cheeks, eyebrows, chin, etc. Small strips of newspaper will help hold these features together and give a good finish coat. Make a little ridge at the bottom of the neck, to hold the clothes on.

Hair can be fashioned with tissue paper. Or paste strips of rug yarn on the head starting with a natural part. The yarn can be braided, tied in a pony tail, or shaped in many other ways.

Now paint the face with poster paint and you are ready for a costume.

Make a costume out of fabric. Add interesting details in keeping with the character. Make sure there is an opening in the back big enough to get your hand through. Run a heavy thread around the neckline with a basting stitch. Tie tightly over the ridge on the neck.

Now, on with the show!

This costume for a clown puppet is basic. For a dress, cut straight across the bottom. For regular pants, cut the legs narrower. Hands and feet are made out of bits of felt which may be stuffed with cotton. Felt can be either sewed or glued. The broken line down from the neckline is cut for an opening for the hand that operates the puppet. Cut this in the back only.

VARIATIONS

Make a puppet head by pasting paper strips over a burned-out light bulb. Use about five to seven layers of newspaper. The features can be built up with tissue just as in the other method. When the paper is thoroughly dry, hit the head sharply against a hard object. This will shatter the glass so that it will fall out, leaving a light, hollow head, perfect for a puppet.

Try making the head over a blown-up balloon. Cover the balloon well with paper strips. Add features and secure with more strips. Then the balloon can be deflated. This kind of head is particularly good fun to do with children. Because of the flexibility of size and variation of shape, many weird, original, and exciting heads can be created. Besides using these heads for puppets, think of the possibilities for party and dance decorations! A gigantic head, or any form that is basically round like a globe, can be built over a blown-up beach ball. Since a beach ball can be expensive, you will want to use it more than once. After the paper strips are dry gently draw out the deflated ball. The opening it leaves can be covered with more strips. The best kind of material to use for a very large ball is building felt.

68

These papier-mâché masks and figures were made by children from five to twelve years old. The masks were made of newspaper over clay. The figure construction was simple. A stick figure armature was made of wire, wrapped with tissue paper and paste, and finished with strips of newsprint paper. Poster paint completed these imaginative and original sculptures.

SOME CLASSROOM PROJECTS

Create scenes to illustrate great historic events.

Make animals two by two for Noah's ark.

Learn the costumes and habits of people of the world. Illustrate with papier-mâché figures or masks.

Describe great moments in literature with papier-mâché scenes.

Create a prehistoric scene, or perhaps one of the interplanetary future.

Create a holiday atmosphere in the classroom with papier-mâché decorations.

Make a float for a holiday parade.

Don't forget the versatility of papier-mâché. Not only can you use paper and paste to create animals and people, but also to build the scenery around them. Contours of the land, hills, and valleys, rocks, stone walls, trees, and buildings can be built with the aid of papier-mâché.

The texture of the paper can often be used just as it dries, as in the case of crumpled newspaper or paper toweling and paste for a rock wall. But don't hesitate to add textural effects over papier-mâché. Sand, salt, sparkle, mica flakes, etc., can be sprinkled over the desired areas while they are still sticky with paste or over paint before it dries.

70

THEATER PROPS

Up to now we have been concentrating on figures and faces, animal and human. There is still another important function for papier-mâché. That is to make props for theatrical productions. These props can also be useful for window displays, dance or party decorations, parade floats, etc. There are many, many possibilities. I will suggest only a few.

Suppose you are a member of a little theater group that is performing a play set in a forest. The backdrop has been painted full of trees with bits of sky peeking through. But the set needs dimension. This can be done by bringing a few trees forward, with perhaps a stump of a tree and some rocks. Obviously it would be impractical to bring trees and rocks into the theater building. So let us make them of papier-mâché.

To begin a tree, nail a long piece of wood (lathe will do) to a baseboard. Around this wrap enough chicken wire to give the tree dimension. Twist and bend the wire so it takes on some of the character of a tree trunk. Now you actually resort to nature. Go to the nearest woods and gather some likely-looking tree branches. Insert these branches into the mesh of the chicken wire at the places where branches would be apt to grow. Secure the branches by wiring or nailing them to the center wood support. Cover the chicken wire with papier-mâché. Twist the

Papier-Mâché

paper from the branches to the main trunk. To get a barklike texture, apply the paper roughly. Crepe paper or paper toweling is particularly good for texture. Paint the tree a dark color and dry brush high lights on the raised surface. Artificial leaves can be wired to the branches. Natural fall leaves last fairly well.

Smaller props such as rocks, tree stumps, and toadstools can be fashioned from the chicken wire without a wood support. Papier-mâché props are light, useful, and durable. They may be used for years. Should they be damaged, they are easily salvaged with a little paste, paper, and paint.

WINDOW
DISPLAYS

The function of a window display is to promote a service or product sold within. Therefore the display should relate to the service or product, or should be sufficiently interesting by itself to make people stop to look. The display could relate to the product, the organization, the season, or holiday, or it can be symbolic. It can relate to copy slogans such as "gentle as a lamb," "quiet as a mouse," "wise as an owl," "fit for a king," etc. A greyhound denotes swiftness; a pig bank, economy; a weight-lifter, strength.

If you intend to work as a free-lance artist making papier-mâché props for window displays, there are several good approaches to acquiring such work.

1. Make several good samples of original papier-mâché objects in the full round and relief. These should be small enough to carry conveniently.

2. Photograph all your jobs. Use these photographs to augment your samples.

3. Make a portfolio of designs and ideas for window displays in which your proposed papier-mâché object becomes an important part of the design.

4. Visit all display departments in your area. Become familiar with the display director. Find out his schedule of activities. You will not be welcome if you arrive on window-changing days.

Merry Christmas

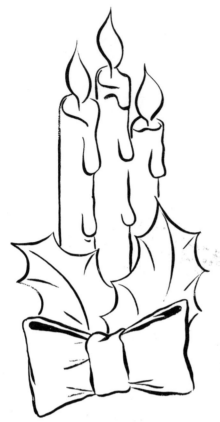

Make it a Merry Christmas with papier-mâché figures or symbols in low relief, half or full round. Use them for home and church decoration, for window displays, gifts, parties, dances, table centerpieces, etc.

Roll large sheets of paper to form tubes for candles. Or use paper tubes. Wire for electricity before adding papier-mâché for texture and other decoration. Candle drips can be made with tissue paper and lots of paste.

Papier-mâché angels are light and may be suspended from the ceiling with a fine wire. To make a village, shape the contours of the hills with chicken wire and cover with large sheets of pasty paper. Secure some of the pieces through the wire so the paper won't lift off when dry. Paint the hills white with tones of blue, and while the paint is still wet spread white sparkle over it to get the gleam of fresh snow. Start the houses with small cereal boxes. Cut to shape, paste or staple together, and finish with papier-mâché details.

78

 # PAPIER-MÂCHÉ CLAY

There is still another way to work with papier-mâché. It is actually the simplest method, but because of its bulk, its use is limited to small objects and handicrafts. I call it the papier-mâché clay method.

This clay is made by tearing quantities of newspaper into small bits. Soak in water until thoroughly saturated. Squeeze and drain off excess water. Then stir into this pulpy mash a thick solution of paste. Knead like dough until thick and pliable like clay.

With papier-mâché clay, small figures may be sculptured around pipe cleaner or wire armatures. Decorative scrolls can be modeled around mirrors, bed headboards, and window

valances. You can make artificial fruit for a horn of plenty. Or make a lamp base by building papier-mâché clay around a bottle or tube.

When the paper is thoroughly dry, it becomes hard like plastic wood. It can be trimmed with a sharp knife and sanded before paint is applied.

PROPORTIONS

I hope I have stressed enough the importance of being creative, of using your imagination and ingenuity, in making such things as masks, figures, and animals. The results of creative imagination are usually more important than the results of formal knowledge. This is particularly true of children's projects. What does it matter then if the eyes of the mask are too high on the face. It doesn't alter the charm of it. If the action and color of a figure are expressive, does it matter if the proportions are wrong? It will just frustrate young children to burden them with rules and theories.

As the child grows older and approaches his teens the reverse is often true. He becomes acutely aware of a lack of knowledge. When he makes a mask, for example, he may be very unhappy with the result because it is poorly proportioned, although he may not realize that that is what disturbs him. An adult who has no art training will want some basic information about proportions to refer to while working out papier-mâché projects.

Fortunately we are created with great variation and individuality ourselves. How dull it would be if we all looked as though we came out of one mold or stepped out of one diagram. We have thin faces, round faces, short noses, long noses. We are thin, fat, short, or tall.

So keeping that in mind, remember that though the diagrams and proportions that follow are presented as facts, they are often necessarily approximate.

The best reference you can get on human anatomy and proportions is your mirror. If you need to know anything about the human figure, stand before a mirror and study your own structure and proportions. Look for relative measurements.

Papier-Mâché

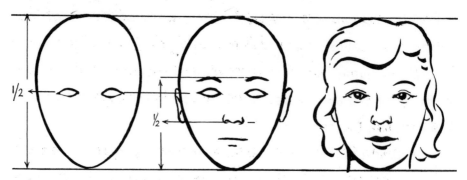

The head is oval or egg-shaped.

The eyes lie halfway between the top of the head and the chin.

The eyes are one eye's distance apart.

The tip of the nose is halfway between the eyebrows and chin.

The ears are parallel to the nose and just past the half of the face, profile view.

The mouth is just above halfway between the nose and chin.

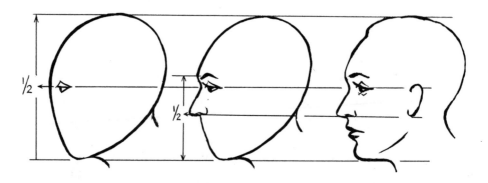

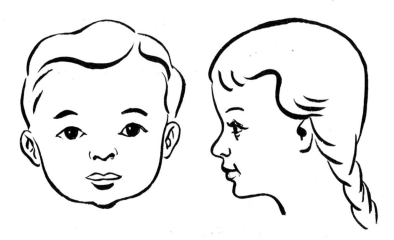

To get a young look, place the eyes lower on the head. The features are small and round; the cheeks are full; the forehead, prominent.

To get an old look, exaggerate structural lines around the eyes, cheekbones, etc. Make expression wrinkles. For a very old look, give the mouth a sunken look.

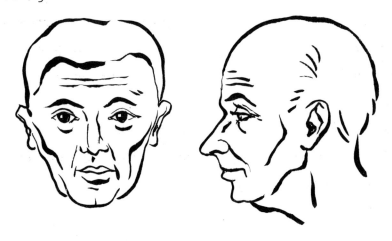

Papier-Mâché

In measuring proportions of a body, the head is considered one unit of measurement.

An adult is seven and one half to eight heads high.

Points to remember:

> First head—chin
> Second head—breast
> Third head—navel
> Fourth head—crotch
> Fifth head—above the knees
> Sixth head—below the knees
> Seventh head—above the ankle

The halfway measurement is where the thigh bone connects to the pelvis, or hip bone.

The knees are halfway between this point and the bottom of the foot.

Notice how your elbow comes just below the waist or to the top of the hip bone. The wrist is at the bottom of the fourth head. Notice, too, the size of the hand. Put your hand in front of your face—it covers it.

The shoulders are about two heads wide.

When the arms are outstretched, they should equal the height of the body.

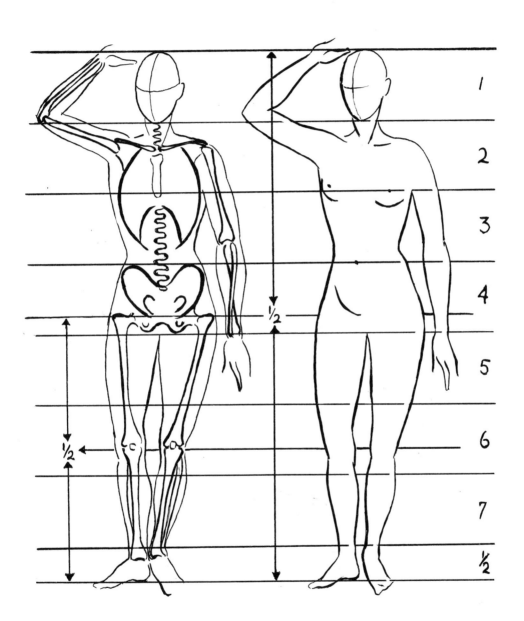

1

2

3

4

½

5

½

6

7

½

Papier-Mâché

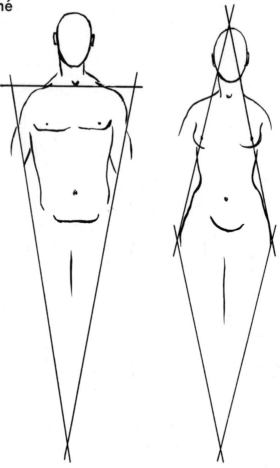

The basic structural differences between an adult male and female figure are the shoulders and hips. The male is broad through the shoulder and narrow through the hips. The female is narrow through the shoulder and wide through the hips. It will help to remember this, if you visualize the male figure in a triangle and the female in a diamond.

86

This sketch shows the comparative proportions from an infant to an adult. The baby is four heads high at birth. The children in the sketch are one, four, eight, and twelve years old.

87

ACKNOWLEDGMENTS

My sincere thanks to my brother, Seymour R. Bass, who took all the step-by-step photographs and many more.

I am indebted also to:

The display directors for whom I made papier-mâché objects and for the use of the photographs of them:

Mr. Jack Dyche, M. Epstein, Morristown, New Jersey

Mr. H. Barrett, R. J. Goerke, Elizabeth, New Jersey

Mr. George W. Browne, Public Service Electric and Gas Co., Newark, New Jersey.

Mr. and Mrs. R. Isley for their help.

Wolin Studio, Summit, New Jersey, for photographs.

And especially to my friend and teacher, Genevieve Karr Hamlin, who helped me (as she did so many others) to understand how to express creativity.